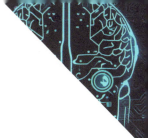

# Mastering GPT-4:
## A Comprehensive Prompt Engineering Guide

A GPT-4 GUIDE
BY GPT-4

# 1. Introduction to GPT-4

## 1.1 Overview of GPT-4 and its capabilities

- GPT-4, or Generative Pre-trained Transformer 4, is an advanced language model developed by OpenAI. It builds upon the success of its predecessor, GPT-3, by offering even greater capabilities in natural language understanding and generation.

- GPT-4 is capable of a wide range of tasks, including text summarization, translation, question-answering, and content generation, among others.

- The model is pre-trained on a massive dataset of text from various sources, allowing it to generate human-like responses based on the input it receives.

## 1.2 Improvements over previous GPT models

- GPT-4 builds upon the advancements of GPT-3, offering even better performance and a wider range of capabilities.

- The model has been trained on an even larger dataset, allowing it to develop a deeper understanding of language and context.

- Architectural improvements and optimization techniques have led to faster and more efficient response generation.

- Enhanced fine-tuning capabilities allow GPT-4 to be more easily adapted for specific tasks or domains.

## 1.3 Real-world applications of GPT-4

- GPT-4's advanced language understanding and generation capabilities have led to numerous real-world applications, such as:

  - Content generation: GPT-4 can create high-quality articles, blog posts, and social media content.

  - Customer support: The model can be used to provide quick and accurate responses to customer inquiries, reducing the workload for human agents.

  - Language translation: GPT-4 is capable of translating text between multiple languages with high accuracy.

  - Education and tutoring: The model can be used to answer questions and provide explanations on various subjects, serving as a valuable resource for students and educators alike.

  - Creative writing and storytelling: GPT-4 can generate compelling narratives, aiding writers in brainstorming ideas or even writing entire stories.

In this introduction, we delved into the advanced language capabilities of GPT-4, a powerful model developed by OpenAI. We examined the improvements over its predecessor, GPT-3, including enhanced performance, broader capabilities, larger training datasets, architectural advancements, and better fine-tuning options. GPT-4's real-world applications encompass content generation, customer support, language translation, education, and creative writing. By understanding its capabilities and effectively crafting prompts, users can harness GPT-4's potential for professional, precise, and tailored outputs that cater to various specific requirements

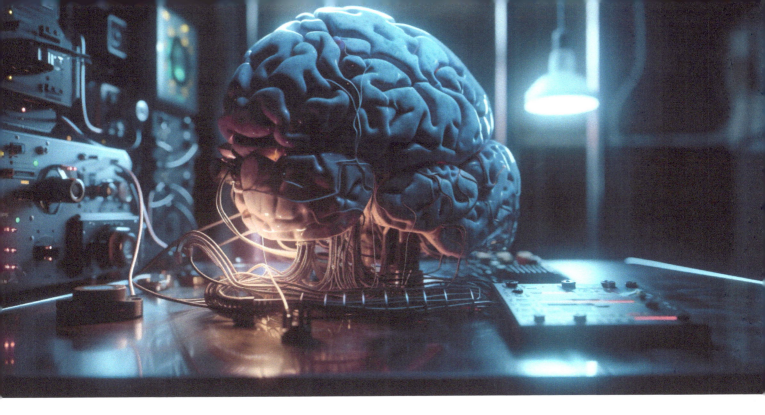

## 2. Understanding Language Models

### 2.1 The basics of natural language processing (NLP)

- Natural language processing (NLP) is a subfield of artificial intelligence (AI) focused on enabling computers to understand, interpret, and generate human language.

- NLP involves a wide range of tasks, such as sentiment analysis, named entity recognition, and language translation.

- Machine learning algorithms, particularly deep learning techniques, play a critical role in advancing NLP capabilities.

### 2.2 How language models work

- Language models are trained to predict the likelihood of a sequence of words appearing in a given context.

- They are typically based on statistical methods or neural networks, with the latter becoming more prevalent due to their ability to capture complex patterns in language.

- Modern language models, like GPT-4, utilize deep learning architectures such as the Transformer, which allows them to handle long-range dependencies and maintain context across large spans of text.

- These models are pre-trained on massive datasets, learning linguistic patterns, grammar, facts, and even some reasoning abilities from the text they process.

## 2.3 GPT-4 architecture and training process

- GPT-4 is based on the Transformer architecture, which relies on self-attention mechanisms to process input sequences in parallel rather than sequentially, resulting in improved efficiency and scalability.

- The model is trained using unsupervised learning, which means it learns to generate text without any labeled data or explicit supervision.

- During the pre-training phase, GPT-4 is exposed to a vast amount of text, learning to predict the next word in a sentence given the words that came before it (masked language modeling).

- This pre-training allows GPT-4 to develop a strong grasp of language structure, context, and even some world knowledge.

- After pre-training, GPT-4 can be fine-tuned on specific tasks or domains using smaller, labeled datasets, enabling it to adapt its capabilities to the specific requirements of an application.

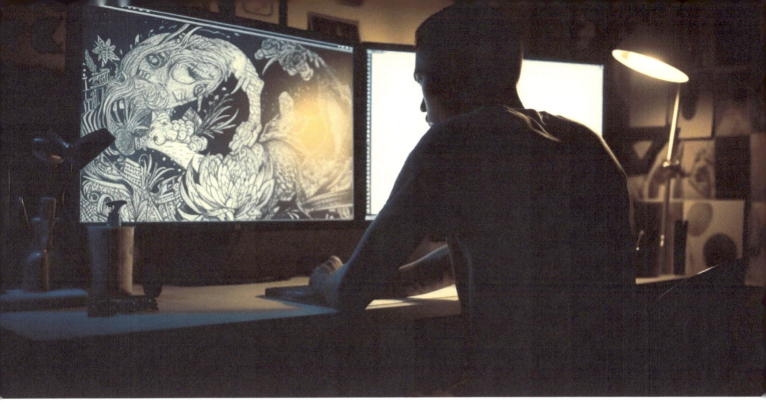

# 3. The Art of Prompt Engineering

## 3.1 Crafting Effective Prompts for GPT-4

### 3.1.1 Understanding GPT-4's Input Structure

- GPT-4 uses a token-based input structure, where a token can be a single character, word, or subword, depending on the language and model configuration.

- The model has a maximum token limit, typically in the range of a few thousand tokens, which must accommodate both the input prompt and the generated response.

- Crafting prompts within this token limit is crucial to ensure the model can generate meaningful and contextually accurate responses.

### 3.1.2 Identifying the Goal of the Prompt

- Before crafting a prompt, it is essential to clearly define the goal or objective you want to achieve with the generated response.

- Goals can vary widely, from generating an article summary or answering a specific question to providing a creative idea or brainstorming solutions to a problem.

- Identifying the goal will guide the prompt's structure, phrasing, and level of specificity.

### 3.1.3 Balancing Openness and Specificity

- Striking the right balance between openness and specificity in a prompt is key to obtaining the desired output.

- Overly specific prompts can limit GPT-4's creativity and reduce the range of possible responses, while overly open prompts can result in vague or unrelated outputs.

- Experimenting with different levels of specificity can help you find the optimal balance for your particular application.

### 3.1.4 Using Natural Language Instructions

- GPT-4 responds well to natural language instructions, making it easier to guide the model's output with conversational prompts.

- Including explicit instructions, such as "summarize the following article" or "translate the following text into French," can help GPT-4 understand the desired outcome more clearly.

- Additionally, you can provide context or background information within the prompt to improve the relevance and accuracy of the generated response.

### 3.1.5 Leveraging System-Level Instructions

- System-level instructions are an advanced prompt engineering technique that can help guide GPT-4's behavior more effectively.

- These instructions can be used to control output length, format, or even the model's "personality."

- For example, you can instruct the model to "explain the topic in simple terms" or "generate a concise summary in bullet points."

### 3.1.6 Iterative Prompt Engineering

- It is essential to approach prompt engineering as an iterative process, refining the prompts based on the quality and relevance of the generated outputs.

- Analyzing the model's responses and identifying areas for improvement can help you modify and fine-tune your prompts for better results.

- Regularly testing and updating your prompts will ensure optimal performance and help you achieve your desired objectives.

In this section, we explored the art of crafting effective prompts for GPT-4, focusing on understanding the input structure, identifying prompt goals, balancing openness and specificity, using natural language instructions, leveraging system-level instructions, and approaching prompt engineering as an iterative process. These principles and techniques are essential for harnessing GPT-4's capabilities and generating professional, technical, precise, and extensive outputs tailored to your specific needs.

## 3.2 Understanding GPT-4's Response Generation

### 3.2.1 Decoding Strategies

- GPT-4 generates responses using various decoding strategies, including greedy search, beam search, nucleus sampling, and temperature-based sampling.

- Greedy search selects the highest probability token at each step but can produce repetitive or non-diverse outputs.

- Beam search expands upon greedy search by maintaining multiple hypotheses, resulting in more coherent outputs but still potentially lacking in diversity.

- Nucleus sampling and temperature-based sampling introduce randomness into the generation process, leading to more diverse and creative outputs at the cost of increased risk of incoherence or irrelevance.

### 3.2.2 Controlling the Length of Generated Responses

- GPT-4's response length can be controlled using parameters such as "max_tokens" or "min_tokens" during the generation process.

- Setting "max_tokens" to an appropriate value can prevent excessively long or verbose responses, while "min_tokens" can be used to ensure a minimum response length.

- Be cautious when setting these limits, as overly restrictive constraints can lead to incoherent or nonsensical outputs.

### 3.2.3 Managing Output Diversity and Creativity

- Output diversity and creativity can be controlled using parameters such as "temperature" and "top_p" during the response generation process.

- Higher "temperature" values result in more diverse and creative outputs, as the model becomes more likely to explore lower-probability tokens.

- The "top_p" parameter, used in nucleus sampling, determines the fraction of total probability mass to consider when selecting the next token. Lower values result in more focused and conservative responses, while higher values encourage more exploration and diversity.

### 3.2.4 Handling Incomplete or Incoherent Responses

- GPT-4's response generation process is inherently probabilistic, which can sometimes result in incomplete or incoherent outputs.

- In these cases, it may be necessary to refine the input prompt or adjust the decoding parameters to improve the quality of the generated responses.

- Additionally, techniques such as response validation or post-processing can be employed to filter out or correct problematic outputs.

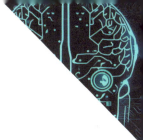

### 3.2.5 Incorporating Domain-Specific Knowledge

- While GPT-4 is pre-trained on a massive dataset and possesses a broad understanding of various topics, it may lack in-depth knowledge of certain domain-specific areas.

- Fine-tuning GPT-4 on domain-specific datasets can improve its performance and relevance in generating responses related to those domains.

- Alternatively, external knowledge sources or APIs can be integrated into the response generation process to augment the model's capabilities and provide more accurate or specialized outputs.

### 3.2.6 Evaluating Generated Responses

- Evaluating the quality and relevance of GPT-4's generated responses is a critical aspect of the prompt engineering process.

- Metrics such as BLEU, ROUGE, and METEOR can be used to assess the performance of GPT-4 in tasks like translation, summarization, or text generation.

- However, these metrics may not fully capture the nuances of human language or the subtleties of the model's output, making human evaluation an essential component of the assessment process.

In this section, we explored GPT-4's response generation process, focusing on decoding strategies, controlling response length, managing output diversity and creativity, handling incomplete or incoherent responses, incorporating domain-specific knowledge, and evaluating generated responses. Understanding these aspects of GPT-4's response generation is crucial for obtaining professional, technical, precise, and extensive outputs tailored to your specific needs and objectives.

## 3.3 Tips and Tricks for Optimizing Prompt Quality

### 3.3.1 Utilizing Prompt Templates

- Developing and using prompt templates can be an effective way to standardize and streamline the prompt engineering process for specific tasks or applications.

- Templates can be adapted and customized as needed, ensuring consistency in the phrasing, structure, and objectives of the prompts.

- Creating a library of prompt templates can save time and effort while maintaining high-quality input prompts across various use cases.

### 3.3.2 Iterative Refinement of Prompts

- As you work with GPT-4, it is crucial to adopt an iterative approach to prompt refinement, analyzing the generated responses and adjusting the prompts accordingly to improve their quality and relevance.

- This process may involve fine-tuning the wording, adding contextual information, or modifying the level of specificity in the prompts.

- Continuously refining your prompts based on the model's performance will help you achieve optimal results and enhance the overall effectiveness of GPT-4.

### 3.3.3 Experimenting with Multiple Prompts

- When attempting to generate a high-quality response for a specific task, it can be beneficial to experiment with multiple prompt variations.

- By testing different phrasings, structures, or instructions, you can identify the most effective prompts for generating the desired output.

- Comparing and analyzing the responses to different prompts can reveal patterns and insights that inform your prompt engineering strategy, leading to improved outcomes.

### 3.3.4 Incorporating User Feedback

- Incorporating user feedback is essential for refining prompts and improving GPT-4's response quality.

- Users can provide valuable insights into the relevance, accuracy, and coherence of the generated responses, which may not be apparent from quantitative evaluation metrics.

- Establishing a feedback loop between users and the prompt engineering process will help you adapt and optimize your prompts to better align with user needs and expectations.

### 3.3.5 Monitoring and Managing Model Drift

- Model drift is a phenomenon where the AI model's performance degrades over time due to changes in the underlying data distribution or user behavior.

- Regularly monitoring GPT-4's performance and output quality is essential for detecting and addressing model drift.

- Strategies for managing model drift include updating the training data, fine-tuning the model, or adjusting the prompt engineering process to account for the changes in user behavior or data.

### 3.3.6 Adapting to Different Language Models

- While GPT-4 is a powerful language model, there may be situations where alternative language models or model architectures are more suitable for specific tasks or applications.

- Adapting your prompt engineering techniques to different language models may require adjusting the input structure, decoding parameters, or domain-specific knowledge integration.

- Developing a deep understanding of the nuances and capabilities of various language models will enable you to apply your prompt engineering skills effectively across different AI systems.

In this section, we delved into tips and tricks for optimizing prompt quality, including utilizing prompt templates, adopting an iterative refinement process, experimenting with multiple prompts, incorporating user feedback, monitoring and managing model drift, and adapting to different language models. Implementing these strategies and techniques will help you craft professional, technical, precise, and extensive input prompts, ultimately enhancing GPT-4's performance and output quality across a wide range of tasks and applications.

# 4. Advanced Prompt Engineering Techniques

## 4.1 Balancing Specificity and Flexibility

### 4.1.1 Understanding the Trade-off

- The balance between specificity and flexibility in prompt engineering is a critical aspect of achieving high-quality, relevant responses from GPT-4.

- Specificity refers to the level of detail, constraints, or explicit instructions in a prompt, while flexibility refers to the degree of freedom granted to the model in generating responses.

- Striking the right balance between these two aspects allows GPT-4 to produce outputs that meet user expectations while remaining adaptable and creative.

### 4.1.2 Benefits of Specificity

- Providing specific instructions, context, or examples in the input prompt can help guide GPT-4 towards generating more relevant and accurate responses.

- Increased specificity can be useful in situations where the desired output adheres to a particular format, structure, or set of guidelines.

- Specific prompts can also help mitigate issues related to incomplete or incoherent responses, as the model is given more explicit guidance on the expected output.

### 4.1.3 Benefits of Flexibility

- Allowing for greater flexibility in prompt engineering can encourage GPT-4 to explore diverse and creative solutions, rather than being constrained to a narrow range of outputs.

- Flexible prompts can be beneficial in situations where the desired response is less rigidly defined or open to interpretation, such as creative writing or brainstorming tasks.

- Providing GPT-4 with more freedom in generating responses can also help reveal unexpected insights or novel perspectives that may not have been anticipated by the user.

### 4.1.4 Techniques for Balancing Specificity and Flexibility

- Experiment with different levels of specificity and flexibility in your prompts to determine the optimal balance for your specific use case.

- Start with a moderately specific prompt and iteratively refine it by either increasing or decreasing the level of specificity, based on the quality and relevance of the generated responses.

- Monitor the impact of these adjustments on GPT-4's output quality, and use the insights gained to inform your prompt engineering strategy.

### 4.1.5 Adapting to Different Tasks and Applications

- The ideal balance between specificity and flexibility may vary depending on the task or application at hand.

- For tasks that require strict adherence to guidelines, such as legal or medical document generation, a higher level of specificity may be necessary.

- Conversely, tasks that involve open-ended problem-solving, brainstorming, or creative expression may benefit from greater flexibility in prompt engineering.

- Continuously adapting your approach to specificity and flexibility based on the unique requirements of different tasks will help you achieve optimal results across various applications.

In this section, we explored the concept of balancing specificity and flexibility in prompt engineering, including understanding the trade-off, recognizing the benefits of specificity and flexibility, learning techniques for finding the right balance, and adapting to different tasks and applications. By mastering the art of balancing specificity and flexibility, you can craft professional, technical, precise, and extensive prompts that guide GPT-4 towards generating high-quality, relevant, and adaptable responses across a wide range of use cases.

## 4.2 Techniques for Controlling Output Length and Format

### 4.2.1 The Importance of Output Control

- Controlling the length and format of GPT-4's generated responses is crucial for ensuring that the outputs meet the specific requirements of various tasks and applications.

- Effective output control techniques can help enhance the relevance, coherence, and readability of the generated text, providing a better user experience and increasing the overall value of the AI system.

### 4.2.2 Controlling Output Length

- To control the output length of GPT-4's responses, you can leverage several techniques:

  - Specify the desired length in the prompt, e.g., "Write a 200-word summary of the following article."

  - Adjust the maximum tokens parameter during the decoding process to limit the response length.

  - Employ post-processing methods to truncate or condense the generated text, ensuring it adheres to the desired length constraints.

- When implementing these techniques, consider the impact on the coherence and relevance of the generated text, as overly restrictive length constraints may lead to incomplete or unclear responses.

### 4.2.3 Controlling Output Format

- To control the format of GPT-4's generated responses, consider the following techniques:

- Provide explicit instructions in the prompt regarding the required format, e.g., "Write a step-by-step guide using bullet points" or "Present the information as a numbered list."

- Incorporate examples or templates in the prompt to demonstrate the desired format, helping guide the model towards generating responses with the appropriate structure.

- Employ post-processing techniques to reformat the generated text, such as converting paragraphs into bullet points, organizing information into tables, or applying consistent styling and formatting rules.

- When applying these techniques, ensure that the format control does not compromise the readability or coherence of the generated text, and maintain a balance between format constraints and the model's creative freedom.

### 4.2.4 Adapting Output Control Techniques to Different Tasks and Applications

- The optimal output control techniques may vary depending on the specific task or application, and it is essential to adapt your approach accordingly.

  - For tasks that require concise summaries or highlights, focus on techniques that effectively control output length while maintaining the coherence and relevance of the generated text.

  - For tasks that involve structured information presentation, such as data analysis, reports, or guides, prioritize techniques that control the output format to ensure the generated text adheres to the required structure and style.

- Continuously refining and adapting your output control techniques based on the unique requirements of different tasks will help you achieve optimal results across various applications.

In this section, we discussed techniques for controlling output length and format in prompt engineering, including understanding the importance of output control, learning methods to control output length and format, and adapting these techniques to different tasks and applications. By mastering these output control techniques, you can create professional, technical, precise, and extensive prompts that elicit high-quality, tailored responses from GPT-4, ensuring that the generated text aligns with the specific requirements of various tasks and applications.

## 4.3 Using System Level Instructions for Better Control

### 4.3.1 Introduction to System Level Instructions

- System level instructions are high-level directives provided within the prompt that help guide GPT-4's behavior throughout the response generation process.

- By incorporating system level instructions in your prompts, you can exert greater control over the model's output, leading to more relevant, coherent, and accurate responses.

### 4.3.2 Benefits of System Level Instructions

- System level instructions offer several benefits in prompt engineering, including:

  - Enhanced control over GPT-4's response generation, helping to achieve desired output characteristics.

  - Improved relevance and accuracy of generated text by guiding the model towards the user's intent.

  - Reduction of potential bias, inaccuracies, or undesirable content in the generated responses.

### 4.3.3 Implementing System Level Instructions

- To incorporate system level instructions in your prompts, consider the following techniques:

  - Set the context: Provide high-level context at the beginning of the prompt to guide GPT-4's understanding of the desired output, e.g., "As an expert in renewable energy, provide an overview of solar power technology."

  - Define the response format: Specify the format or structure that the generated response should follow, e.g., "Present your response as a series of bullet points."

- Impose constraints: Impose specific constraints on the model's response generation process, such as avoiding certain topics, sources, or language, e.g., "Do not mention any political opinions in your response."

- Encourage critical thinking: Instruct GPT-4 to consider multiple perspectives or evaluate the credibility of information before generating a response, e.g., "Analyze the advantages and disadvantages of the proposed solution."

- Experiment with different combinations of system level instructions to identify the most effective strategies for achieving the desired output characteristics in various tasks and applications.

### 4.3.4 Balancing System Level Instructions and Model Autonomy

- While system level instructions offer better control over GPT-4's output, it is essential to maintain a balance between these directives and the model's creative autonomy.

  - Overly restrictive system level instructions may limit the model's ability to explore diverse solutions or generate novel insights.

  - Conversely, insufficient guidance through system level instructions may result in outputs that are less relevant, coherent, or accurate.

- Strive to find an optimal balance between system level instructions and model autonomy by iteratively refining your prompts and observing the impact on the generated responses.

In this section, we discussed using system level instructions for better control in prompt engineering, including understanding the benefits of system level instructions, implementing these instructions in your prompts, and balancing system level instructions with model autonomy. By effectively incorporating system level instructions, you can create professional, technical, precise, and extensive prompts that guide GPT-4 towards generating high-quality, tailored responses that align with user intent and adhere to desired output characteristics across a wide range of tasks and applications.

# 5. GPT-4 Applications in Various Domains

## 5.1 Business Applications: Customer Support and Content Generation

### 5.1.1 Overview of Business Applications

- GPT-4 has vast potential in the business domain, particularly in customer support and content generation, where its advanced natural language understanding and generation capabilities can significantly enhance efficiency, user experience, and overall effectiveness.

### 5.1.2 Customer Support

- GPT-4 can revolutionize customer support by:

  - Automating responses to frequently asked questions, reducing response times and freeing up human support staff to handle more complex queries.

  - Identifying and escalating critical issues to human support staff based on keywords, sentiment analysis, or severity of the issue.

  - Providing personalized support by leveraging the model's understanding of user preferences, purchase history, or other context-specific factors.

- Integrating seamlessly with existing customer support platforms, such as chatbots, helpdesks, and CRMs, to streamline support processes and improve user satisfaction.

- When using GPT-4 for customer support, it is essential to ensure the model is fine-tuned for the specific domain and optimized for prompt engineering techniques discussed earlier, ensuring accurate, relevant, and coherent responses.

### 5.1.3 Content Generation

- GPT-4 can significantly impact content generation in businesses by:

  - Producing high-quality, engaging content for various formats, such as blog posts, articles, social media updates, and newsletters, tailored to the target audience and aligned with the brand's voice and style.

  - Generating content in multiple languages, facilitating global outreach and expanding the business's audience.

  - Enhancing creativity and ideation by generating alternative versions, headlines, or perspectives on a given topic, which can inspire new ideas and foster innovation.

  - Streamlining the content creation process by providing templates, outlines, or summaries, reducing the time and effort required for content development.

- When leveraging GPT-4 for content generation, ensure the model is fine-tuned for the specific industry, target audience, and content format, and apply advanced prompt engineering techniques to achieve optimal output quality, relevance, and coherence.

In this section, we explored GPT-4 applications in business, focusing on customer support and content generation. By understanding the potential of GPT-4 in these areas and applying the advanced prompt engineering techniques discussed earlier, businesses can harness the power of GPT-4 to enhance efficiency, user experience, and overall effectiveness across a wide range of tasks and applications.

## 5.2 Creative Applications: Storytelling and Brainstorming

### 5.2.1 Overview of Creative Applications

- GPT-4's advanced natural language understanding and generation capabilities offer a wealth of opportunities in creative applications, particularly in storytelling and brainstorming, where the model can generate imaginative, coherent, and engaging content that captivates audiences and stimulates innovative thinking.

### 5.2.2 Storytelling

- GPT-4 can revolutionize storytelling by:

  - Generating original stories in various genres, styles, and formats, ranging from short stories and novellas to screenplays and interactive narratives.

  - Crafting compelling characters, dialogue, and plotlines that resonate with the target audience and evoke emotional responses.

  - Adapting existing stories or concepts into new formats or mediums, such as turning a novel into a screenplay or creating a graphic novel adaptation.

  - Providing feedback on story drafts, identifying areas for improvement, and suggesting alternative plot points or character developments to enhance the narrative.

- When using GPT-4 for storytelling, ensure the model is fine-tuned for the specific genre, style, and target audience, and apply advanced prompt engineering techniques to achieve optimal output quality, coherence, and engagement.

### 5.2.3 Brainstorming

- GPT-4 can significantly impact brainstorming in creative domains by:

  - Generating a diverse range of ideas, concepts, and solutions to address specific challenges or explore new opportunities, stimulating innovative thinking and fostering a culture of creativity.

  - Providing alternative perspectives or approaches to a given problem or topic, encouraging critical thinking and collaborative problem-solving.

  - Identifying trends, patterns, or insights from large datasets, such as market research, social media analytics, or user feedback, which can inform creative decision-making and strategy development.

  - Facilitating ideation sessions, such as virtual workshops or focus groups, by generating prompts, questions, or scenarios that encourage participants to think outside the box and explore new possibilities.

- When leveraging GPT-4 for brainstorming, ensure the model is fine-tuned for the specific domain, problem, or audience, and apply advanced prompt engineering techniques to achieve optimal output quality, relevance, and diversity.

In this section, we explored GPT-4 applications in creative domains, focusing on storytelling and brainstorming. By understanding the potential of GPT-4 in these areas and applying the advanced prompt engineering techniques discussed earlier, creative professionals and organizations can harness the power of GPT-4 to generate imaginative, coherent, and engaging content that captivates audiences, stimulates innovative thinking, and enhances the overall creative process across a wide range of tasks and applications.

## 5.3 Educational Applications: Tutoring and Question-Answering

### 5.3.1 Overview of Educational Applications

- GPT-4's advanced natural language understanding and generation capabilities offer significant opportunities in the field of education, particularly in tutoring and question-answering, where the model can provide personalized learning experiences, enhance knowledge retention, and facilitate mastery of complex subjects.

### 5.3.2 Tutoring

- GPT-4 can revolutionize tutoring by:

  - Providing personalized, one-on-one instruction tailored to the learner's individual needs, learning style, and proficiency level.

  - Explaining complex concepts and ideas in a clear, concise, and accessible manner, using examples, analogies, and visualizations to aid understanding.

  - Offering real-time feedback on learners' progress, identifying areas for improvement, and adjusting instructional strategies accordingly.

  - Supplementing traditional learning resources, such as textbooks and lectures, with interactive, adaptive learning materials that engage learners and promote active learning.

- When using GPT-4 for tutoring, ensure the model is fine-tuned for the specific subject, educational level, and learner profile, and apply advanced prompt engineering techniques to achieve optimal output quality, relevance, and pedagogical effectiveness.

### 5.3.3 Question-Answering

- GPT-4 can significantly impact question-answering in educational contexts by:

  - Responding accurately and promptly to learners' questions, providing detailed explanations, examples, and supplementary resources to facilitate understanding.

  - Identifying gaps in learners' knowledge and generating targeted questions that encourage critical thinking, problem-solving, and deeper learning.

  - Integrating with existing learning management systems, discussion forums, and chat platforms to offer seamless, context-aware question-answering support.

  - Assisting educators and researchers in addressing queries related to course content, research methodologies, or data analysis, enabling them to focus on higher-order tasks and decision-making.

- When leveraging GPT-4 for question-answering, ensure the model is fine-tuned for the specific domain, context, and audience, and apply advanced prompt engineering techniques to achieve optimal output quality, accuracy, and coherence.

In this section, we explored GPT-4 applications in education, focusing on tutoring and question-answering. By understanding the potential of GPT-4 in these areas and applying the advanced prompt engineering techniques discussed earlier, educators, learners, and educational institutions can harness the power of GPT-4 to provide personalized learning experiences, enhance knowledge retention, and facilitate mastery of complex subjects across a wide range of educational contexts and applications.

# 6. Quality Assessment and Improvement of GPT-4 Outputs

## 6.1 Assessing GPT-4 Responses for Accuracy and Relevance

### 6.1.1 Overview of Response Assessment

- Ensuring the accuracy and relevance of GPT-4's responses is critical for obtaining reliable and useful results in various applications. This section outlines a systematic approach for assessing the quality of GPT-4 outputs and implementing feedback loops to improve the model's performance over time.

### 6.1.2 Accuracy Assessment

- To assess the accuracy of GPT-4's responses, follow these steps:

  - Establish a set of evaluation criteria or benchmarks, such as factual correctness, logical consistency, and domain-specific expertise, to measure the quality of GPT-4's responses.

  - Develop a test dataset comprising representative prompts and corresponding ground truth answers, ensuring diversity in question types, domains, and difficulty levels.

- Evaluate GPT-4's responses against the ground truth answers using appropriate evaluation metrics, such as accuracy, F1-score, or mean reciprocal rank (MRR), to quantify the model's performance.

- Analyze errors and inaccuracies in GPT-4's responses to identify patterns or biases, and use this information to fine-tune the model or adjust prompt engineering strategies accordingly.

### 6.1.3 Relevance Assessment

- To assess the relevance of GPT-4's responses, follow these steps:

  - Define relevance criteria that align with the target application or user requirements, such as topic alignment, user intent matching, or actionability.

  - Develop a test dataset comprising representative prompts and corresponding relevance judgments, ensuring diversity in user intents, contexts, and preferences.

  - Evaluate GPT-4's responses against the relevance judgments using appropriate evaluation metrics, such as precision, recall, or normalized discounted cumulative gain (NDCG), to quantify the model's performance.

  - Analyze instances of low relevance in GPT-4's responses to identify patterns or shortcomings, and use this information to fine-tune the model or adjust prompt engineering strategies accordingly.

### 6.1.4 Continuous Improvement and Feedback Loops

- Establish feedback loops to continuously improve GPT-4's response quality by:

  - Collecting user feedback on GPT-4's responses, including ratings, comments, or error reports, to gain insights into the model's strengths and weaknesses.

  - Periodically re-evaluating GPT-4's performance using updated test datasets and relevance judgments, accounting for changes in user requirements, domain knowledge, or application contexts.

  - Implementing iterative model fine-tuning and prompt engineering adjustments based on evaluation results and user feedback, and monitoring the impact of these changes on GPT-4's response quality.

In this section, we outlined a systematic approach for assessing GPT-4 responses for accuracy and relevance and implementing feedback loops for continuous improvement. By following these steps and applying the advanced prompt engineering techniques discussed earlier, developers, researchers, and organizations can ensure the reliability and usefulness of GPT-4 outputs across a wide range of tasks and applications, ultimately enhancing the overall performance and utility of the model in various domains.

## 6.2 Iteratively Refining Prompts for Better Results

### 6.2.1 Overview of Iterative Prompt Refinement

- The process of iteratively refining prompts is crucial for obtaining better results from GPT-4. By continuously fine-tuning prompts based on the model's responses and user feedback, you can optimize the quality, relevance, and usefulness of GPT-4 outputs across diverse applications.

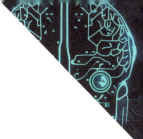

### 6.2.2 Steps for Iterative Prompt Refinement

- To refine prompts iteratively for better results, follow these steps:

  - Develop an initial set of prompts based on the target application, user requirements, and domain-specific knowledge, applying the advanced prompt engineering techniques discussed earlier.

  - Evaluate GPT-4's responses to the initial prompts, assessing their accuracy, relevance, and other quality dimensions, as outlined in Section 6.1.

  - Identify areas for improvement in GPT-4's responses, such as response length, specificity, or topical focus, and modify the prompts accordingly. This may involve adjusting the phrasing, adding or removing keywords, or using system-level instructions.

  - Repeat Steps 2 and 3 in an iterative manner, refining the prompts based on GPT-4's responses and user feedback, until the desired response quality, relevance, and utility are achieved.

### 6.2.3 Strategies for Effective Prompt Refinement

- To optimize prompt refinement, consider the following strategies:

  - Experiment with different prompt variations, such as rephrasing questions, using alternative keywords, or specifying desired response formats, to identify the most effective prompts for eliciting the desired GPT-4 outputs.

  - Leverage user feedback, particularly when refining prompts for complex, ambiguous, or subjective queries, to ensure that GPT-4's responses align with user expectations and requirements.

  - Monitor the impact of prompt refinements on GPT-4's response quality, tracking improvements or regressions in accuracy, relevance, and other quality dimensions, to inform subsequent refinement iterations.

### 6.2.4 Balancing Refinement Efforts with Model Limitations

- When refining prompts, it is essential to recognize and account for GPT-4's inherent limitations, such as biases, knowledge gaps, or inconsistencies. Be prepared to adjust your expectations and prompt refinement strategies accordingly, and consider supplementing GPT-4's outputs with additional information sources or expert validation when necessary.

In this section, we outlined a systematic approach for iteratively refining prompts to achieve better results with GPT-4. By following these steps and applying the advanced prompt engineering techniques and strategies discussed earlier, developers, researchers, and organizations can optimize the quality, relevance, and utility of GPT-4 outputs across a wide range of tasks and applications, ultimately enhancing the overall performance and value of the model in various domains.

## 6.3 Limitations of GPT-4 and Potential Pitfalls

### 6.3.1 Overview of GPT-4 Limitations

- Despite its impressive capabilities, GPT-4 has inherent limitations and potential pitfalls that users should be aware of. Understanding these limitations is crucial for effectively employing GPT-4 in various applications and managing user expectations accordingly.

### 6.3.2 Key Limitations and Potential Pitfalls

1. Knowledge gaps and outdated information: GPT-4's knowledge is based on the training data available up to a specific date, and it may lack information on more recent events, updates, or advancements. Users should verify the correctness and timeliness of GPT-4's responses, particularly for time-sensitive or rapidly evolving domains.

2. Bias and controversial content: GPT-4 may generate responses that reflect biased perspectives, stereotypes, or controversial viewpoints, as it learns from a diverse range of sources with varying levels of reliability and objectivity. Users should be cautious when using GPT-4 for sensitive topics and consider implementing filtering mechanisms to minimize the risk of generating inappropriate content.

3. Ambiguity and vagueness: GPT-4 may produce ambiguous or vague responses, particularly when faced with complex, open-ended, or multi-faceted questions. Users should employ advanced prompt engineering techniques, such as specifying desired response formats or providing context, to elicit more focused and informative outputs from GPT-4.

4. Inconsistency and contradiction: GPT-4 may generate responses that are inconsistent or contradictory, either within a single response or across multiple responses to similar prompts. Users should be vigilant in detecting such inconsistencies and consider refining their prompts or seeking additional information sources to resolve contradictions.

5. Over-optimization and overfitting: While refining prompts can improve GPT-4's response quality, excessive fine-tuning or over-optimization may lead to overfitting, where the model becomes too specialized for specific prompts and loses its ability to generalize across diverse queries. Users should balance the prompt refinement process with the need to maintain GPT-4's flexibility and adaptability across various tasks and domains.

### 6.3.3 Mitigating Limitations and Potential Pitfalls

- To address GPT-4's limitations and potential pitfalls, consider the following strategies:

  - Implement robust evaluation and feedback loops, as discussed in Sections 6.1 and 6.2, to continuously assess and improve GPT-4's response quality, relevance, and utility.

  - Employ advanced prompt engineering techniques and iterative refinement processes to optimize GPT-4's performance for specific tasks, domains, and user requirements.

- Supplement GPT-4's outputs with additional information sources, expert validation, or user feedback, particularly for complex, ambiguous, or sensitive topics, to ensure the reliability and appropriateness of the generated content.

In this section, we outlined the key limitations and potential pitfalls of GPT-4, as well as strategies for mitigating these issues. By understanding and addressing these limitations, developers, researchers, and organizations can effectively employ GPT-4 in various applications while managing user expectations and ensuring the reliability, relevance, and utility of the generated outputs.

# 7. Ethical Considerations and Responsible Use of GPT-4

## 7.1 Overview of Ethical Concerns

- As with any advanced AI technology, using GPT-4 raises ethical concerns that developers, researchers, and organizations must consider to ensure responsible and beneficial outcomes. In this section, we discuss key ethical considerations related to GPT-4 and provide guidelines for its responsible use.

## 7.2 Key Ethical Considerations

1. Privacy and data security: Ensuring the privacy and security of user data is paramount when using GPT-4. Users should implement appropriate data protection measures, such as encryption, access controls, and secure storage, to prevent unauthorized access, disclosure, or misuse of sensitive information.

2. Bias and fairness: As mentioned in Section 6.3, GPT-4 may generate biased or controversial content, which can have negative consequences for users and society. Users should actively address biases in GPT-4's outputs through prompt engineering, filtering mechanisms, and user feedback, striving for fair and unbiased AI-generated content.

3. Transparency and accountability: Users should be transparent about the use of GPT-4 in their applications, disclosing its role in generating content, recommendations, or decisions, and being accountable for its outputs. This may involve providing explanations, justifications, or context for GPT-4's responses and addressing user concerns or inquiries as needed.

4. Misinformation and disinformation: GPT-4's ability to generate realistic and persuasive content can be exploited for spreading misinformation or disinformation. Users should ensure that GPT-4-generated content is accurate, reliable, and well-sourced, and should be cautious when using GPT-4 for topics prone to misinformation or manipulation.

5. Intellectual property and copyright: GPT-4 may generate content that resembles or incorporates existing copyrighted works, raising intellectual property concerns. Users should respect copyright laws and consider implementing mechanisms to detect and prevent potential copyright infringements in GPT-4-generated content.

## 7.3 Guidelines for Responsible Use of GPT-4

To ensure the ethical and responsible use of GPT-4, users should adhere to the following guidelines:

1. Follow best practices for prompt engineering, quality assessment, and iterative refinement, as outlined in previous sections, to optimize GPT-4's performance and mitigate potential pitfalls and limitations.

2. Actively address and monitor biases, fairness, and controversial content in GPT-4's outputs, employing prompt engineering techniques, filtering mechanisms, and user feedback to ensure unbiased and appropriate AI-generated content.

3. Be transparent and accountable in using GPT-4, disclosing its role in content generation, providing explanations or context for its outputs, and addressing user concerns or inquiries as needed.

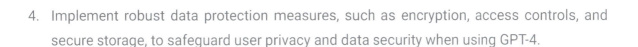

4. Implement robust data protection measures, such as encryption, access controls, and secure storage, to safeguard user privacy and data security when using GPT-4.

5. Comply with applicable laws, regulations, and ethical standards, including intellectual property and copyright laws, and consider the potential societal and individual impacts of GPT-4-generated content.

By adhering to these guidelines and addressing the ethical considerations discussed in this section, developers, researchers, and organizations can harness the power of GPT-4 responsibly, ensuring beneficial outcomes for users, stakeholders, and society at large.

# 8. Future Directions and Research Opportunities in GPT-4 Applications

## 8.1 Fine-tuning GPT-4 for Specific Tasks and Domains

### 8.1.1 Introduction

- In this section, we discuss the process of fine-tuning GPT-4 for specific tasks and domains, which enables the development of more targeted and effective AI-powered applications. We cover the benefits of fine-tuning, the steps involved, and best practices for successful implementation.

### 8.1.2 Benefits of Fine-tuning

1. Improved performance: Fine-tuning GPT-4 on domain-specific or task-specific data can lead to better performance and higher-quality output, as the model becomes more specialized in handling the nuances and intricacies of the target domain or task.

2. Reduced computational resources: Fine-tuning can help reduce the computational resources required for training and inference, as a smaller, more specialized model can be more efficient than a larger, more generalized one.

3. Enhanced customization: Fine-tuning allows for greater customization, enabling the development of AI applications that cater to specific user needs, preferences, and requirements.

### 8.1.3 Steps for Fine-tuning GPT-4

1. Define the target task or domain: Clearly identify the specific task or domain for which the GPT-4 model will be fine-tuned, ensuring that it aligns with the desired application's goals and objectives.

2. Collect and preprocess data: Gather relevant, high-quality data for the target task or domain, ensuring it is representative, diverse, and free of biases. Preprocess the data to ensure it is compatible with GPT-4's input requirements.

3. Split the data: Divide the data into training, validation, and test sets, maintaining an appropriate balance to enable effective model training and evaluation.

4. Fine-tune the model: Train the GPT-4 model on the task-specific or domain-specific data, adjusting hyperparameters and model architecture as needed to optimize performance.

5. Evaluate performance: Assess the fine-tuned model's performance on the validation and test sets, using appropriate evaluation metrics and benchmarks to gauge its effectiveness and suitability for the target task or domain.

6. Iterate and refine: Based on the evaluation results, make adjustments to the fine-tuning process, data, or model configuration, and repeat the process as needed to achieve the desired performance level.

### 8.1.4 Best Practices for Fine-tuning GPT-4

1. Use transfer learning: Leverage GPT-4's pre-trained weights and knowledge as a starting point for fine-tuning, capitalizing on its vast understanding of language and ability to generalize across tasks.

2. Monitor overfitting: Be mindful of overfitting during the fine-tuning process, particularly when working with small or noisy datasets. Regularize the model and employ techniques such as dropout or early stopping to mitigate this issue.

3. Experiment with hyperparameters: Explore various hyperparameter settings, such as learning rate, batch size, and model architecture, to find the optimal configuration for the target task or domain.

4. Incorporate domain-specific knowledge: Consider incorporating domain-specific knowledge, such as expert rules or heuristics, into the fine-tuning process to further enhance the model's performance and understanding of the target domain.

By following these steps and best practices, developers can successfully fine-tune GPT-4 for specific tasks and domains, unlocking the full potential of the technology and enabling the creation of more powerful, targeted, and effective AI applications.

## 8.2 Integrating GPT-4 with Other AI Technologies

### 8.2.1 Introduction

- In this section, we explore how GPT-4 can be integrated with other AI technologies to create more advanced, versatile, and powerful applications. We discuss the benefits of integration, various integration scenarios, and best practices for successful implementation.

### 8.2.2 Benefits of Integrating GPT-4 with Other AI Technologies

1.  Enhanced capabilities: Combining GPT-4 with other AI technologies can result in more comprehensive and sophisticated applications that leverage the strengths of multiple AI components to perform complex tasks.

2.  Improved performance: Integrating GPT-4 with complementary AI technologies can lead to better overall system performance, as each component can focus on its area of expertise and contribute to a more effective solution.

3.  Scalability: Integrating GPT-4 with other AI technologies can help build scalable systems that can handle a variety of tasks and adapt to changing requirements.

### 8.2.3 Integration Scenarios

1.  GPT-4 with Computer Vision: Combining GPT-4's natural language processing capabilities with computer vision technologies can enable applications such as image captioning, visual storytelling, and visual question answering.

2.  GPT-4 with Speech Recognition and Synthesis: Integrating GPT-4 with speech recognition and synthesis systems can enable voice-based AI applications, such as virtual assistants, transcription services, and voice-controlled devices.

3.  GPT-4 with Reinforcement Learning: Pairing GPT-4 with reinforcement learning algorithms can lead to intelligent systems capable of learning from interactions with their environment, enabling applications like autonomous robots and adaptive recommendation systems.

4.  GPT-4 with Knowledge Graphs: Combining GPT-4 with knowledge graph technologies can enable AI systems that can reason over structured data, allowing for more advanced question-answering, information retrieval, and decision-making applications.

### 8.2.4 Best Practices for Integrating GPT-4 with Other AI Technologies

1. Define clear interfaces: Establish well-defined interfaces between GPT-4 and the other AI components to ensure seamless communication and data exchange.

2. Leverage modularity: Design the integrated system in a modular manner, allowing for easy replacement or modification of individual components without disrupting the overall system functionality.

3. Optimize data flow: Ensure efficient data flow between GPT-4 and the other AI components, minimizing latency and maximizing throughput to enhance overall system performance.

4. Monitor and evaluate system performance: Continuously monitor and evaluate the performance of the integrated system, identifying bottlenecks and opportunities for improvement to optimize the overall solution.

5. Maintain compatibility: Ensure compatibility between GPT-4 and the other AI technologies, both in terms of software and hardware requirements, to facilitate smooth integration and operation.

By integrating GPT-4 with other AI technologies and following these best practices, developers can create more advanced and powerful AI applications, unlocking the full potential of these cutting-edge technologies and driving innovation across various domains.

## 8.3 Future Developments and the Impact on Prompt Engineering

### 8.3.1 Introduction

- In this section, we discuss the anticipated future developments in AI and their potential impact on prompt engineering for GPT-4 and similar language models. We explore the trends, challenges, and opportunities that lie ahead, and how they will shape the way we design and engineer prompts.

### 8.3.2 Trends in AI and Their Impact on Prompt Engineering

1. Increasing Model Complexity: As AI models become more complex, prompt engineering will need to evolve to accommodate the intricacies of these advanced systems. This may require developing more sophisticated techniques for crafting effective prompts and a deeper understanding of the underlying model architecture.

2. Enhanced Contextual Understanding: With improvements in AI's ability to understand context, prompt engineering will need to focus on leveraging this enhanced contextual awareness to create more accurate and relevant prompts that can effectively guide AI models.

3. Personalized AI: As AI systems become increasingly personalized, prompt engineering will need to adapt to create individualized prompts that cater to the specific needs, preferences, and context of each user.

4. Multimodal AI: The growing trend of multimodal AI systems, which integrate various data types like text, images, and audio, will necessitate the development of new prompt engineering techniques that can effectively manage and utilize these diverse data sources.

### 8.3.3 Challenges and Opportunities in Future Prompt Engineering

1. Ethical Considerations: As AI systems become more advanced and pervasive, prompt engineering will need to grapple with the ethical implications of AI-generated content and the potential for manipulation or misuse. This may involve creating guidelines, safeguards, and best practices for responsible prompt engineering.

2. Explainability and Transparency: With the increasing complexity of AI models, understanding how they generate responses becomes more challenging. Future prompt engineering will need to address issues of explainability and transparency, ensuring that users can trust and understand the AI-generated outputs.

3. Real-time Adaptation: As AI systems become more dynamic and capable of learning from user interactions, prompt engineering will need to develop techniques for real-time adaptation of prompts, allowing AI models to continually refine and improve their performance.

4. Collaboration with Other AI Technologies: As discussed in the previous section, the integration of GPT-4 with other AI technologies will require prompt engineering to evolve, ensuring that prompts can effectively guide and control the combined AI system.

### 8.3.4 Preparing for the Future of Prompt Engineering

1. Stay Informed: Keep up-to-date with the latest developments in AI research, technology, and applications to anticipate and prepare for the changing landscape of prompt engineering.

2. Experiment and Iterate: Continuously experiment with new prompt engineering techniques and strategies, learning from both successes and failures to refine and improve your approach.

3. Foster Collaboration: Collaborate with other AI practitioners, researchers, and stakeholders to share insights, knowledge, and best practices in prompt engineering, fostering innovation and driving the field forward.

4. Embrace Ethical Responsibility: Actively consider the ethical implications of prompt engineering and strive to develop responsible and transparent practices that prioritize user trust and safety.

By staying informed, experimenting with new techniques, collaborating with others, and embracing ethical responsibility, prompt engineers can prepare for and navigate the exciting future developments in AI and their impact on prompt engineering for GPT-4 and similar language models.

## 9. Exhibit A: Optimized GPT-4 Prompts

### 1.  Factual Question:

- Suboptimal Prompt: "Who wrote Hamlet?"

- Optimized Prompt: "Please provide the name of the author who wrote the famous play 'Hamlet'."

### 2.  Creative Writing:

- Suboptimal Prompt: "Write a story."

- Optimized Prompt: "Compose a short story of about 500 words, set in a medieval kingdom, with a protagonist who discovers a hidden magical power."

### 3.	Recipe Generation:

- Suboptimal Prompt: "Give me a recipe."

- Optimized Prompt: "Provide a detailed recipe for a vegetarian pasta dish that serves four people, incorporating ingredients such as tomatoes, garlic, basil, and olive oil."

### 4.	Advice:

- Suboptimal Prompt: "How to be happy?"

- Optimized Prompt: "Could you provide five practical and actionable steps that an individual can take to improve their overall happiness and well-being?"

### 5.	Debate:

- Suboptimal Prompt: "Pros and cons of AI."

- Optimized Prompt: "Please present three well-argued points in favor of the development and use of artificial intelligence, and three well-argued points against it, considering the potential societal, economic, and ethical implications."

### 6.	Educational Explanation:

- Suboptimal Prompt: "Explain photosynthesis."

- Optimized Prompt: "Provide a clear and concise explanation of the process of photosynthesis, suitable for a high school biology student, including the key components involved and the role of sunlight in this process."

## 7.  Brainstorming:

- Suboptimal Prompt: "Ideas for a party."

- Optimized Prompt: "Generate a list of 10 creative and engaging party theme ideas for a 30th birthday celebration, considering the preferences of a diverse group of guests."

## 8.  Personalized Recommendation:

- Suboptimal Prompt: "What book should I read?"

- Optimized Prompt: "Considering my preference for science fiction novels with strong female protagonists and thought-provoking themes, can you recommend a book that I would likely enjoy?"

## 9.  Historical Events:

- Suboptimal Prompt: "Tell me about World War II."

- Optimized Prompt: "Provide a concise overview of World War II, including its primary causes, major participants, key events, and the ultimate outcome of the conflict."

## 10.  Career Guidance:

- Suboptimal Prompt: "How to choose a career?"

- Optimized Prompt: "What are five important factors an individual should consider when choosing a career path, and how can they assess their skills, interests, and values to make an informed decision?"

## 11.  Travel Recommendations:

- Suboptimal Prompt: "Where should I go on vacation?"

- Optimized Prompt: "Given my preference for cultural experiences, historical sites, and local cuisine, recommend a travel destination that would offer a unique and memorable vacation experience."

## 12. Technical Troubleshooting:

- Suboptimal Prompt: "My computer is slow."

- Optimized Prompt: "I am experiencing slow performance on my Windows 10 computer. Can you suggest a step-by-step approach to diagnose and resolve common issues that may be causing this problem?"

## 13. Language Learning:

- Suboptimal Prompt: "Teach me Spanish."

- Optimized Prompt: "Provide five essential Spanish phrases for a beginner, including their English translations and a brief explanation of when and how to use each phrase in a conversational context."

## 14. Movie Review:

- Suboptimal Prompt: "Review a movie."

- Optimized Prompt: "Provide a well-rounded review of the 2010 science fiction film 'Inception,' directed by Christopher Nolan, discussing its plot, visual effects, acting, and overall impact on the genre."

## 15. Business Strategy:

- Suboptimal Prompt: "How to start a business?"

- Optimized Prompt: "Outline a step-by-step process for launching a successful online e-commerce store, including market research, product selection, branding, website development, and marketing strategies."

## 16.    Fitness Routine:

- Suboptimal Prompt: "Give me a workout plan."

- Optimized Prompt: "Design a four-week workout plan for a beginner, focusing on full-body strength training and cardiovascular exercise, with clear guidance on exercise selection, frequency, and progression."

These optimized prompts for GPT-4 provide more specific context, clear instructions, and tailored information to guide the model in generating accurate, relevant, and useful responses.

## Conclusion

This comprehensive guide to mastering GPT-4 provides valuable insights into the world of natural language processing and language model optimization. We've covered the fundamentals of GPT-4, its architecture, and its many practical applications. By understanding the art of prompt engineering, crafting effective prompts, and using advanced techniques for better control, you can harness the full potential of GPT-4 in a wide range of domains.

We've also addressed the importance of ethical considerations, responsible AI use, and the future of prompt engineering in the rapidly evolving landscape of AI technologies. As you continue to explore the fascinating world of GPT-4 and its many applications, always remember the principles of ethical AI development and usage.

For more information and resources on AI, language models, and GPT-4, I invite you to visit www.rmutt.es. My website offers a wealth of knowledge, tips, and tools to help you navigate the ever-evolving landscape of artificial intelligence and stay up-to-date with the latest developments in the field.

I hope this guide has been an invaluable resource on your journey towards mastering GPT-4, and we look forward to seeing the innovative ways you apply these skills and techniques to your projects and endeavors.